Can You Guess?

Ann H. Matzke

ROURKE PUBLISHING
www.rourkepublishing.com

www.rourkepublishing.com

PHOTO CREDITS: Cover, Page 22: © Rob Belknap; Title Page: © Skip ODonnell; Page 3, 17: © Jack Hollingsworth; Page 4: © Marko Lazarevic; Page 5: © Yuri Arcurs; Page 7: © Vladimir Voronin; Page 8: © Robo123; Page 9: © Kitsen; Page 11: © Alexan24; Page 12: © Sonya Etchison; Page 13: © Andres Rodriguez; Page 15: © Derek Dammann; Page 16, 18, 19; © Ivonne Wierink; © Michael Flippo; Page 20: © Björn Magnusson; Page 21: © Rohit Seth; Page 23: © digitalskillet

Edited by Kelli L. Hicks

Cover and Interior design by Tara Raymo

Library of Congress Cataloging-in-Publication Data

Matzke, Ann H.
Can you guess? / Ann H. Matzke.
  p. cm. -- (Little world math concepts)
Includes bibliographical references and index.
ISBN 978-1-61590-295-8 (Hard Cover)(alk. paper)
ISBN 978-1-61590-534-8 (Soft Cover)
1. Mathematical notation--Juvenile literature. 2. Mathematical notation. I. Title.
QA41.M36 2011
519.5'44--dc22

                                                2010009278

Rourke Publishing
Printed in the United States of America, North Mankato, Minnesota
033010
03301OLP

www.rourkepublishing.com - rourke@rourkepublishing.com
Post Office Box 643328 Vero Beach, Florida 32964

Guessing an amount is estimating.
You guess, is it *more* or is it *less*.

How many blocks make a house?

I guess three. What's your guess, *more or less?*

Did you guess *less*? It takes just two.

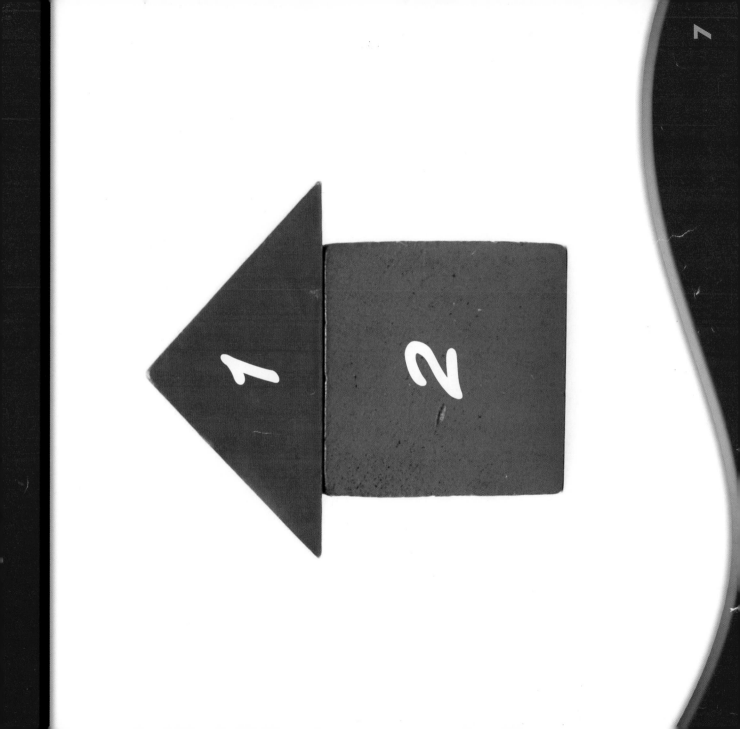

How many pieces of chalk fit in the box?

I guess six. What's your guess, more or *less?*

Did you guess more? It takes eight.

How many steps to cross the finish line?

I guess seven. What's your guess, *more or less?*

Did you guess more? It takes about nine.

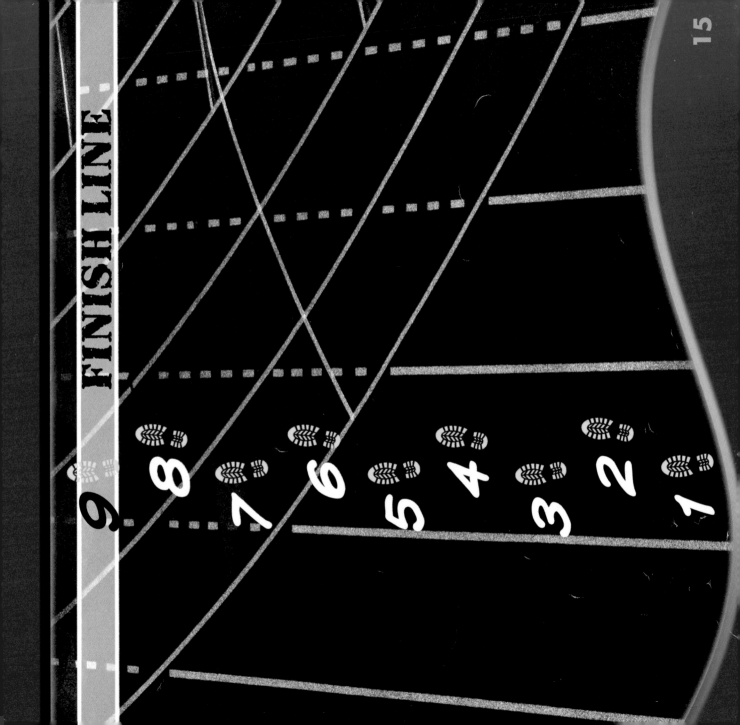

FINISH LINE

9 8 7 6 5 4 3 2 1

How many pails of sand fill a bucket?

I guess eleven. What's your guess, more or less?

Did you guess *less?* It takes about eight.

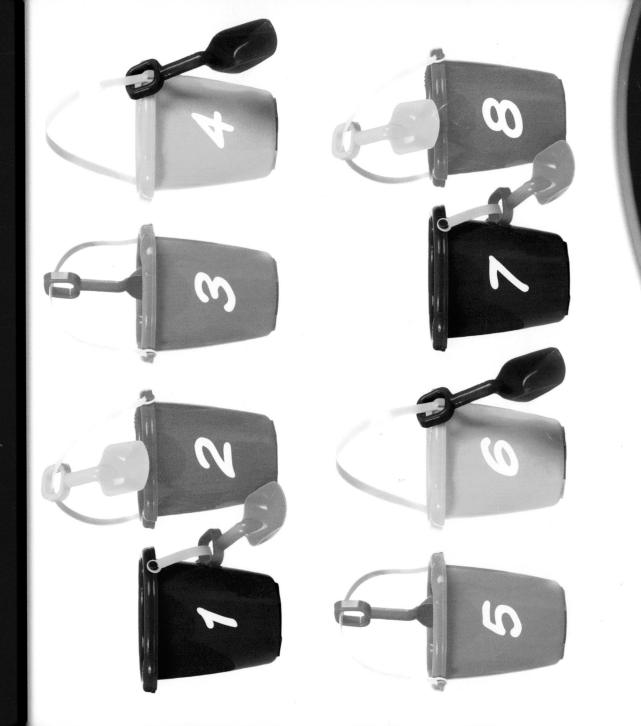

How many gumballs are in the jar?

I guess twelve. What's your guess, more or less?

Did you guess more? It takes about fifteen.

Both *more* and *less* are good guesses!

Index

Websites

www.ixl.com/math/practice/grade-1-estimate-to-the-nearest-ten

www.ixl.com/math/practice/grade-2-guess-the-number

www.education.com/worksheets/all-grades/?q=by+the+shore

www.teacher.scholastic.com/max/candy/index.htm

www.ngfl-cymru.org.uk/vtc/ngfl/ngfl-flash/estimate/estimate.html

About the Author

Ann Matzke is an elementary library integration specialist who loves to estimate. Ann often has estimating games set up in the school library for her students. Ann lives in Gothenburg, Nebraska near an original Pony Express Station and enjoys reading and writing.